THIS BOOK BELONGS TO:

_____

THIS BOOK IS DEDICATED TO ALL THE POLICEMEN, POLICE WOMEN AND FUTURE POLICE.

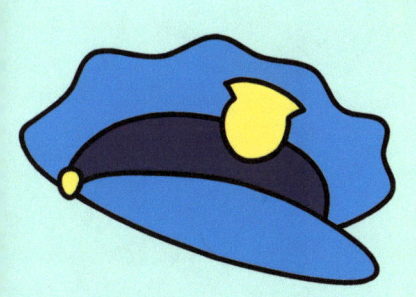

This book is dedicated to my children - Mikey, Kobe, and Jojo.

Copyright © 2024 Grow Grit Press LLC. All rights reserved. No part of this book may be reproduced in any form without permission in writing from the publisher. Please send bulk order requests to info@ninjalifehacks.tv

Paperback ISBN: 978-1-63731-951-2
Hardcover ISBN: 978-1-63731-953-6
eBook ISBN: 978-1-63731-952-9

Printed and bound in the USA.
NinjaLifeHacks.tv

Ninja Life Hacks®
by Mary Nhin

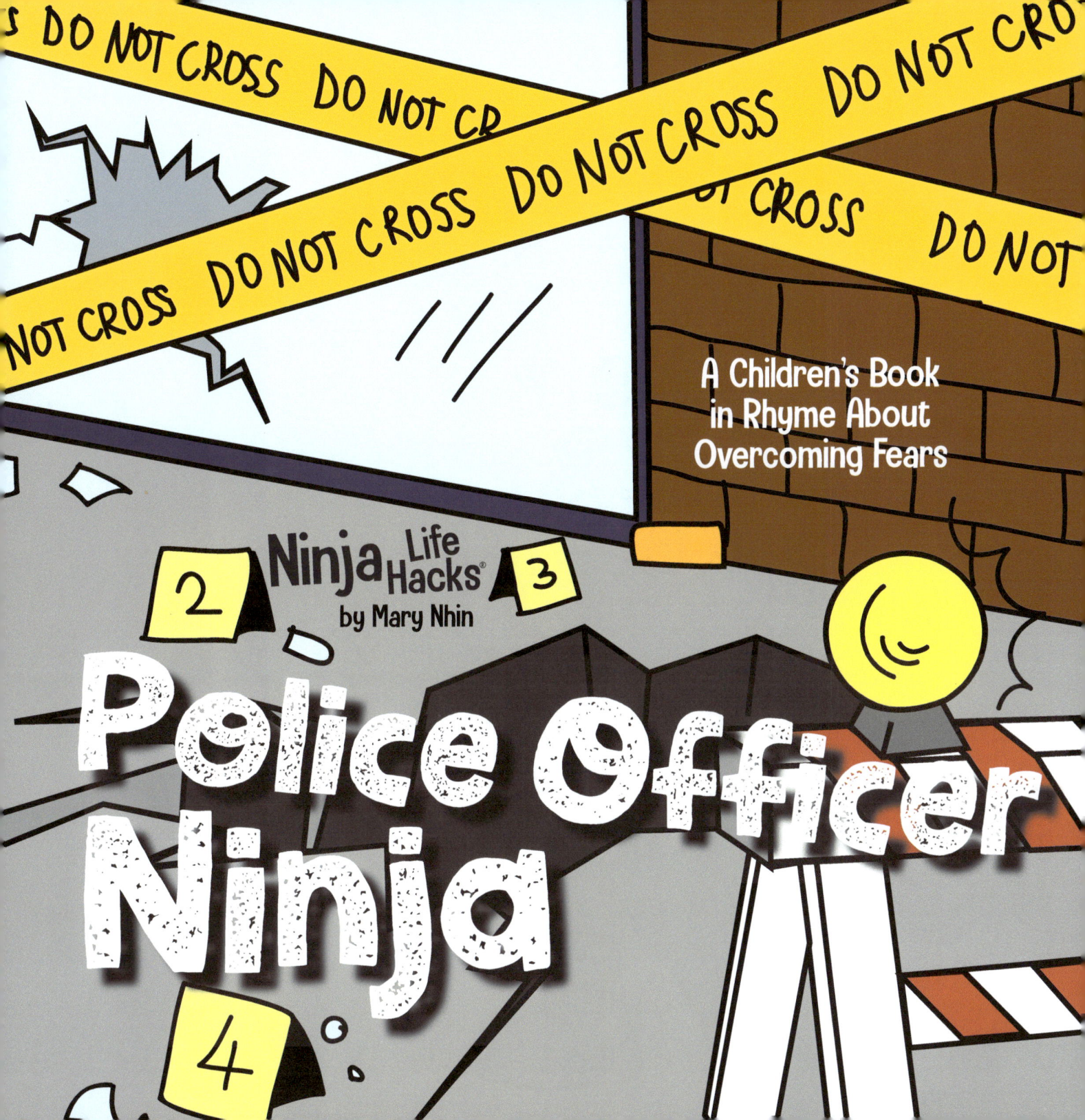

Now when I patrol,
Both night and day,
I know it's okay
To feel this way.

Check out the fun Police Officer Ninja lesson plans at ninjalifehacks.tv

I love to hear from my readers. Email me your feedback or thoughts on what my next story should be at info@ninjalifehacks.tv   Yours truly, Mary

 @marynhin   @GrowGrit
#NinjaLifeHacks

 Ninja Life Hacks

 Mary Nhin   Ninja Life Hacks

 @officialninjalifehacks

Police Officer Ninja Craft Activity

Materials Needed:

- Paper plates (one per child)
- Police officer and ninja templates (included below)
- Markers, crayons, or colored pencils
- Glue
- Scissors
- Black construction paper (for the ninja mask)
- Optional: Stickers or decorative items

Instructions:

1. **Color the Templates:**
   - Give each child a set of templates (Police Officer Hat and Police Badge).
   - Have them color the templates according to their preference. Encourage creativity—let them use different colors and designs!

2. **Prepare the Paper Plate:**
   - Take the paper plate and color it as the background for their Police Officer Ninja's face. They can make it look like a ninja's face or a police officer's face.

3. **Create the Police Officer Hat:**
   - Cut out the police officer hat from the template.
   - Glue the hat to the top of the paper plate. This will be the hat of their Police Officer Ninja.

4. **Attach the Police Badge:**
   - Cut out the police badge from the template.
   - Glue the badge onto the paper plate, either on the ninja's chest area or somewhere that stands out.

5. **Decorate and Personalize:**
   - Let the children add their own personal touches to their Police Officer Ninja by drawing additional details, adding stickers, or using other decorative items.

6. **Show and Tell:**
   - Once the crafts are complete, have a "show and tell" session where each child can share their Police Officer Ninja with the group and explain their creative choices.

www.ingramcontent.com/pod-product-compliance
Lightning Source LLC
Chambersburg PA
CBHW041711160426
43209CB00018B/1802